Do I Have a Gizzard?

Learning from Children

Martha Jean Stewart

Published by AKA-Publishing
Columbia, Missouri
www.aka-publishing.com

Book design by Yolanda Ciolli
www.yolandaciolli.com

ISBN 978-1-936688-09-8

Do I Have a Gizzard?

Learning from Children

Martha Jean Stewart

Foreword

The days my three children were exploring the world and arriving at insightful conclusions are long past. I was so busy preparing nutritious food, keeping them clothed, and answering streams of questions that I had no time left for recording their creative moments.

It is different with my grandchildren.

I started keeping a list of their clever stories on my computer and listened carefully to phone calls which started with "Guess what happened today?"

Then I sorted through my old letters, journals and descriptions of play dates to add the adventures of Justin, Beth, Luke, Ellie and Zora to my collection. I began embellishing each story and drawing conclusions from them.

May you too enjoy and reflect on the stories that opened vistas of vision to our world. May your heart be moved by the inclusion of the last story in my book.

—Martha Jean Stewart

Table of Contents

Part One: Twists of Interpretation

Table of Contents

Part Two: Sno Cones and Other Stories

Part Three: Dragons and Such

Table of Contents

Table of Contents

Part Four: Expanding Thoughts Through Travel

The Old Yellow Couch

Part One

Twists

of

Interpretation

1

The New Bird Feeder

Three-year old Justin sat on his mother's lap, looking out their picture window at the birds coming to inspect their new bird feeder. All kinds of birds milled around the imposing structure that Santa Claus had brought—soaring birds, chattering birds, colorful birds and bedraggled birds. They circled and fluttered about in the sky as they surveyed the shiny, new contraption attached to the balcony of their house. It looked somewhat like a castle with a golden crown, mounted on a red foundation with shiny loops for perches. The inside of the feeder was filled with an assortment of seeds. The birds surveyed the feeder, first with one eye and then the other. They circled closer, and soon a few got up the courage to settle on the perches and taste the seeds.

Mother Angel's lesson began. "Do you know how birds eat? See their mouths with little beaks instead of lips. The birds look at a seed and attack it with the point of their beak. They swallow the seed whole, for they have no teeth like we have. The seed goes into their bodies and travels to their gizzard. The gizzard is a muscle that is open in the middle like our fist which grinds up seeds using the little rocks that the birds eat with their food. After the seeds are crushed, they can be digested."

Justin looked puzzled, then thoughtful, and finally ever so pleased as he lifted his shirt, bared his chest and asked enthusiastically, "Do I have a gizzard?"

"No, you have teeth," answered his mother quietly. "You don't need a gizzard."

Justin sat looking ever so thoughtful with his head tilted aside. Suddenly he straightened up, beamed, and proclaimed, "My sister Baby Beth has a gizzard. She doesn't have any teeth."

Life begins by sorting through explanations
and drawing correct conclusions.

2

Beth's First Day of School

First days of school are exciting events for everyone—children, parents, and teachers. The classroom is set up to appeal to the interests of children. Parents discuss the wonderful things that happen at school. Children focus on getting ready for the first day of school. There's a shopping adventure to purchase a new dress and hair band to match, a back-pack like the ones big kids carry, a lunch box with animals painted on it, and of course, new crayons, paste, scissors and Kleenex.

Bravery is the first order of the day. Beth was delivered to kindergarten with assurance that all would go well. Shy Beth put her things away and watched the other children play. Her mother could hardly wait for her to come home. The report at the end of the day came through in grand style. "Well, I didn't cry! I thought about it a couple of times, but I didn't." A comforting hug made her feel quite self-sufficient.

We learn to control our emotions
by choosing important tasks to fill our lives.

3

The Joy of Independence

How exciting to hear a child's first words of independence! "I will do it by myself." Ellie was a do-it-myself kind of gal. Her petite stature made her assertions even more unbelievable. When she took a bath, it took getting into the tub three times before she made it by herself. The first time she slithered around and fell into the water. I pulled her arm up. She promptly got out of the tub, stood beside me and informed me in no uncertain terms that she would get in the tub by herself. I watched, but when she started slipping, I reached out and touched her back, only to find her bopping out of the tub again, informing me that "I will do it by myself." I gave up and let her slide under the water and surface, grinning with, "I did it."

After the bath, we went into the kitchen for a snack. She grabbed a banana and informed me, "I will peel it by myself, but you can take off its nose."

A spirit of self-determination
helps us conquer life's perplexities.

4

Zora's Bedtime

A bedtime ritual calls for music and a story. Mother picks a song, and Zora joins in, learning the words to many songs. One night, Zora took charge and suggested, "I will sing a song, and you can sing with me." She started her song, making up words as she went along. "Sing, sing," she admonished her mother. "Listen to me. You sing!"

Her Mother thought humming would suffice, but alas, she made up the tune to go with the random assortment of words.

In frustration, Zora finally announced, "No one knows how to sing with me."

We have to learn the songs of others
before we can sing with them.

5

Fabricated Bedtime Stories

A dutiful parent can come across a bit didactic at times. Teresa is no exception, but Luke has a way of bringing her back to reality. Bedtime is a quiet time that involves a story telling adventure.

Teresa features noble Sir Luke in many bedtime stories. Sir Luke has no guns, cannons, shields or bows and arrows. He must contrive to out-fox his enemies with his wit. He uses such things as marshmallows, glue, and string to capture the evil knights of the kingdom. Every night Sir Luke is embellished with more ingenuity.

All went well, or so Teresa thought, until one night Luke asked pensively, "Mom, do you think brave Sir Luke could meet some real knights with real bows and arrows and have a real fight?"

Another night Luke suggested, "Tell me a story of knights and volcanoes. Make it at least a five volcano story."

We learn to use our ingenuity
to make life's stories exciting.

6

A Policeman's Visit

The policeman came in full regalia ready to convince every preschooler that a policeman's job is the most wonderful vocation in the world. He asked some leading questions which raised a clamor that never subsided.

Luke took over. "If a bad man came along, I would hit him, and I'd have my mother hit him. She is very strong."

Soon everyone's mother was strong and brave and could knock down every bad guy and kick as well.

The policeman gave up and finally agreed to come back another day.

Action for handling bad guys calls for
creative measures—and strong mothers.

7

A Broken Toy

Disgruntled about a toy from Miner Mikes that didn't work, tired Beth complained for twenty minutes on her way home from the Lake of the Ozarks. Finally her Mother admonished her, "Now Beth you have complained for twenty minutes. That is enough. Put your disgruntled thoughts out of your mind and think about something pleasant."

Beth quickly retorted, "Now Mama, you don't understand. I have a thought in my head about a broken toy. I can't think of two thoughts at the same time. It is not easy to get rid of one thought when you already have it in your head. Don't you know that?"

How does one replace
a bad thought with a good one?

8

Dad's Race

Luke watched his Dad exercising vigorously. He seemed to attach importance to the task. Luke watched him thoughtfully and finally exploded, "Why do you do this every day?" Luke asked.

"Well, I plan to enter a race," Brian answered.

Then the barrage of questions began. "What race? Where will it be? How long will it be? How many people will be in it? Now, Dad, are you going to win this race?"

Brian responded, "Oh, I don't think so."

Quickly Luke interrupted with a soothing tone in his voice, "Oh, that's all right, Daddy. We'll still be so proud of you."

We learn the value of encouragement
at an early age.

9

Why do I have to Sleep?

Sleep strategies are an important game all parents and children play. After being put to bed, Ellie reported that first she would "need to eat, then read, and last I will cry."

~~~

Luke insisted he was hungry in the middle of the night. Finally his tired mother got up and offered to get whatever he wanted to eat, but informed him that he had to eat whatever he chose.

She prepared the food. He looked at it and decided he wasn't hungry after all. His mother pressured him to eat what he had chosen.

His explanation followed, "I like the food, but my tongue doesn't like it."

~~~

"I can't take a nap because I'm nocturnal," Luke informs the world.

~~~

"It's light. Time to get up. It's morning. Open your eyes," chimed Ellie at the first peep of dawn.

~~~

Beth likes to awake early and lie babbling in her bed. She scolds anyone who tries to pick her up, but then lays her head down on a comforting shoulder and pats it.

~~~

"Now Luke, no more questions! It is past time for you to go to sleep."

"Oh, Mom, someday my kids will have all kinds of questions for me, and I had better start figuring out the answers."

~~~

Beth volunteered that she had a very good idea. "Why couldn't we all wear pajamas that match and all sleep in the same bed?"

~~~

Just tell Beth she doesn't have to take a nap, but she does have to rest two minutes with her eyes closed. Experience tells us she will be out for two hours.

~~~

Luke explains that he needs to be carried to bed because his knees are getting old and really hurt.

~~~

Teresa gave Luke orders about taking a nap. "Your job is to close your eyes and go to sleep. Do you understand?"

"Oh, indubitably," three-year old Luke responded.

"What?" questioned Teresa.

"Indubitably," said Luke, "like on Winnie the Pooh."

~~~

Luke decided he had grown up and informed his mother, "You know, I don't think I need "moo-moo" or a blanket any longer. I just don't need them. If I get afraid, I'll just think about really good things like…God and love of my family."

~~~

After Teresa put Luke down for a nap, in a few minutes he reported that he felt so good. "I have had a good nap."

**We learn that sleep soothes
the cares of the world.**

10

Big Zan

"Mom, there's a new boy at school named Zan who pushes me around.   You know bigger kids just think that they can push me."

Mom offered a sympathetic, "Yes," and asked a teaching question, "What can you do to handle the situation?

"Well, I can move backwards, but that makes me feel bad." Luke answered.

Mom offered her usual advice, "Did you try using your words to tell him how pushing made you feel?"

"Now, Mom, do you think big kids are going to listen? Big kids think they are better because they think big is better, but big is just big and little is just little. Sometimes little is better because they don't push kids around. Daddy was little. Our family tries to choose what is right, but it seems so exciting to be big and tough."

Learning to handle the pushers
in the world is not an easy task.

11

A Century's Worth of Popcorn

Justin came home from his first Blue and Gold Boy Scout Banquet walking on air.   He had received a badge, a patch, a medal, and had won a sleeping bag for selling the most popcorn.

It doesn't get much better than that.   He announced to the world, "Pa and Neanie will have plenty of popcorn for the century."

Hyperbolic statements
underline possibilities.

12

Representation

When learning that indeed she would be moving from a private school into the public school system, Beth confronted her parents with, "But I don't have any representation. In a democracy people get to vote on important decisions, and you didn't give me any representation."

**We learn democratic
principles early in America.**

13

Questions, Questions, Questions!

Luke's questions don't need answers, only a listener.

"Did you know that a mama praying-mantis is larger than a daddy praying-mantis? Isn't that amazing? Usually daddies are bigger than mamas."

~~~

"Butthead is not a good thing to call someone, but it's a cool thing to *do*, especially if you are a dinosaur."

~~~

"We don't say, "Ding-dong dumb bell, shut up. It is much better to say, 'Quiet down guys.'"

~~~

"Do ghosts really melt?"

~~~

"I need a construction hat at school. The fact of the matter is the walls might fall down. I saw Aaron push on the walls. You never can tell. It is an old building."

~~~

"If grocery stores shut down, do you think we could go hunting?"

~~~

"There's Big K. I wonder where Little K is?"

~~~

"Did you know dinosaurs died off before human beings came? When do you think human beings will die off? I wonder who will come after human beings die off."

~~~

"Do you think Pa and Neanie are old enough to know Paul Revere?"

~~~

"How did people know how to make letters?"

~~~

"There are more rules than I can keep up with like—company first—please and thank you—use your nice voice—pick it up and clean it up—never hit—take a bath—get dressed—use sunscreen—ask first—and don't kill."

~~~

"Wow! Santa is really a good listener."

~~~

When Luke was dressed up for a wedding, Teresa complimented him on how handsome he looked.

Philosophical Luke responded, "Well, I really would like to look pretty on the inside too," then paused and added, "I wonder if Pa and Neanie will come to my wedding when I get married, or will they be dead?"

Observations are the sparks
that ignite the beginning of wisdom.

14

School Awards

Beth, upon receiving the All-School-Award as the Shooting Star for first grade queried her mother, "You mean New Haven School is going to give me an award for first grade after I cried every day for a month?"

Aren't we glad teachers
look for possibilities in students?

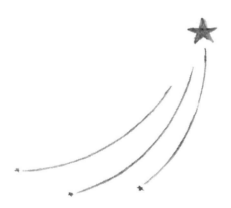

15

Buzz Light Year

Eleanor doesn't waste effort with words when gestures will suffice. She brought her Buzz Light Year toy to Teresa and made a big effort to punch the button that made Buzz talk. Then she found a button on her dress, showed her mother and punched the button on the dress.

Teresa articulated an explanation of the difference in buttons. Eleanor chugged away quite happy to have Teresa confirm the difference.

Oh, that all explanations
about the world were that simple.

16

The Draft

In reading a history story to Luke, Daddy Brian read about the draft.

Luke stopped him to ask, "What is the draft?"

Brian launched into an explanation and concluded by stating that Pa was drafted and had to go to Korea.

Luke looked puzzled and had trouble sorting out the rationale of Pa's response to the draft. Finally, Luke exploded, "Well, why was Missouri upset with Korea?"

Our tangle of war webs
is never easy to sort through.

17

Day-Dreaming

Luke sees no need to hurry through life when it is much more fun to saunter and talk, or just day-dream. He is quite happy to be the last one in line, the last one to put his coat on to go home, and the last one to dress in the morning. Teresa continues to try to get him to school on time.

Once she told the teacher that he would most probably come to school some day in his pajamas. His teacher assured her that he wouldn't be the first child to do so.

Finally one day, Teresa started suggesting that she and Ellie would just have to leave for school without him. That brought a response that cut Teresa short.

"Mom, do you know how that makes me feel when you tell me you may go off and leave me? Don't you know that all that does is make me worry that you will leave without me? It just looks like you could find a kinder way of saying things."

We always need to work on finding kinder
and more tactful ways to get our points across.

18

Gloating

Angel came bringing Beth after school with a snack and left her with the grandparents at Cedar Lake while she took Justin to his after-school lesson.

When Angel returned with Justin, his ice cream in hand, Beth was concerned that she should have ice cream like his.

Her mother reminded her that she had her treat earlier.

All Beth could do was use words to put Justin in his place, "Justin, are you gloating?"

Angel had given her children a lecture about gloating earlier in the week. Justin hid his gloating in short order.

Life has so many lessons to learn,
even a simple one like gloating.

19

A Telephone Call

One day we received a special phone call, "Pa, would you like to have Ellie tell you what she saw today?"

"Pa, I saw three fucks, a fire fuck, a dump fuck, and a police fuck."

***Getting all the letters right
in words takes practice.***

20

When Someone is Sick—Help!

One Sunday morning Glen stayed home from church because he had been vomiting.

At the last minute Beth hesitated about getting into the car to go to Sunday School. Suddenly she turned and flew into the house. She opened the cabinet door, grabbed a Tupperware bowl, ran up to the bedroom, handed her dad the bowl with instructions, "If you get sick, Daddy, you can throw up in this."

Mission accomplished, she ran back to the car, pleased that she had done for her dad what her mother did for her when she was sick.

We learn to be compassionate
by experiencing compassion.

21

Why do we have to know that?

The kindergarten teacher's techniques came under Luke's scrutiny. "Well, why should I bother to get work done early when she just gives me more? Today she had a whole new computer program just for me."

"I don't know how to make my numbers. I can't write to 50. Who wants to bother to write numbers in a row? She gave me problems with six numbers. She wanted to see if I could do them."

"I don't know my letters. I don't like to write them. She even had me read a book to her."

Luke's teacher reports that Luke always asks, "Why do we need to do that? Why do we need to know that? Is there another way we could do it? Is this the best way?"

Oh, that we might know what is
the best way to accomplish every task!

22

Lunch

Dad greeted Luke with, "Say, Luke did you have a good day at school? What did you have for lunch?"

Luke responded with, "Now, Dad, how can you expect me to remember that? Don't you know my brain is really a factory of ideas? My brain is going non-stop. Do you know that my brain has gone non-stop for a year?"

"Well, Luke," Dad said, "I just wanted to know what you had for lunch."

Sometimes we can make
simple things seem so complicated.

23

Love

A morning snuggle session can set up a philosophic discourse on love, especially for Luke. "Oh, mom, I just love our family. I wish our family was bigger. Nancy and Ken are going to have another baby. I wish we would have another baby. I would help take care of it. When are Ken and Nancy going to have their baby?"

Teresa explained that their baby was due to be born in three months, and it takes nine months to grow a baby.

Luke was undaunted, "Well, Mom, I bet if you tried really hard you could beat Nancy and Ken."

Thinking of possibilities is always fun,
well, most of the time.

24

Sharing

Mother Angel took five-year-old Justin to the barbershop for a haircut. After a long wait, the task was finally completed. She bought him candy for a treat and informed him, "This is for your patience and endurance. Remember, Justin, you need to share this treat with Beth when you get home."

With a twinkle in his eyes, he responded, "Of course, for I am a loving and caring brother."

***Humor can turn sharing
into a gracious act.***

25

Departing

Teresa and the children took Daddy Brian to the airport to leave for a week's seminar. Ellie was terribly sad that Dad could not hold her.

Feeling Ellie's sadness, Luke informed Teresa, "I really feel sad inside."

Teresa explained, "Well, let's think. When you are a dad, and you have to go on a trip, what do you think you could do to make your little boy and girl not feel so sad?"

Luke answered forcefully, "Well, when I am a daddy, I'm going to stay at home. Their mother can go out and work and earn the money, but I am staying home. I will probably have eight kids, and I will stay home with all of them."

***Solutions to problems are simple
when projected into the future.***

26

Conversation of Three-Year-Olds

A conversation between Luke and his friend Nick on the way to the Art Museum goes something like this:

"We are getting bigger and bigger."

"Now we are three."

"Yeah, next we'll be four, then five, then six."

"Then our parents will die off. First your bones get achy and your knees hurt."

"Then your body hurts."

"Yeah. But you won't die off. That will be another twelve years."

"Yeah."

"Will Dr. Seuss be at the museum?"

"No, he died."

"How did he die?"

"He was old."

"Well, someone could have chopped his head off."

Speculation starts at an early age.

27

Glitter Glue

Luke had a wonderful time working with glitter glue. He finished his project, and his mother cleaned up the mess. In doing so, she threw a scrap of paper with a dab of glitter in the waste basket. When Luke saw the scrap thrown away, he protested, "No, you cannot throw that away, Mom."

Teresa countered with, "Now Luke, you can't save every scrap piece of paper."

Luke set her straight by explaining, "Mom, you just need to understand that it is just the kind of person I am. I save all my scraps."

All persons are measured
by their idiosyncrasies.

28

Company Manners

It's hard work teaching children company manners.

Playtime was not going well, so Teresa motioned for Luke to come for a little talk.

Luke wished to avoid the private lecture, so he suggested, "Why don't you tell me what it is about? Well, why not give me an idea?"

After the discussion of the confrontation that was brewing, Luke laid out the whole problem.

"We were playing office, and Jake announced he was going to be the boss of everything, but I am bigger and older."

Wouldn't it be good if we could count on people
who are bigger and older to have all the answers?

29

Hair Pulling

After an altercation with Ellie, Luke pulled Ellie's hair.

Teresa sent him up to his bedroom for time out.

Sometime later, Luke came downstairs and gave Ellie a special toy. Teresa complimented Luke with, "Oh, Luke, I am so proud of you."

Luke thought a moment and replied, "Well, I did it because I needed to feel proud of myself."

Oh, if only time-outs could
solve the problems of the world.

30

The Magic of Chores

There's a magic about chores supervised by grandparents.

Pa invited Justin to help him build a deck on his house. Justin came early in the morning and was put to work staining boards.

They both worked all day with paint brushes, boards, and hammers. Putting stain on a real board was much more exciting than coloring a picture in a coloring book. Can you believe only a little stain got on Justin's clothes?

Justin reflected afterwards, "There are just so many things to do at Pa and Neanie's house."

Justin came once to visit and demanded to know, "Where is your de-doubler? I want to use it."

"What is a de-doubler?" I asked.

"That thing I used last week."

"Oh, the cone brush with an extension handle that we used to knock down the spider webs. It's in the garage."

We had spiders building massive webs under our balcony. Justin de-doubled all their webs and gave a lecture to Beth who was a little afraid of spiders.

Capturing the fun of chores
feeds the work ethic we teach.

31

Climbing

We met for breakfast at the new McDonalds with an indoor play area of multiple levels.

Three-year-old Beth's latest ploy was to climb up as high as she could on her own, wait until a bigger kid came along, and say, "Help, pease."

A mother standing beside the slide instructed her child to help the little girl down.

"Oh, no," Angel assured the mother. "She wants to go to the top so she can come down the big slide."

Early in life we learn that help enables us
to conquer the big slides in life.

32

A Lengthy Explanation

A few days after joining her older brother Justin in a multi-level class room, Beth reported that Justin was smarter. "He just knows more."

Angel sought to console Beth with a lengthy mother-daughter talk about her own days in third grade, when she got terribly upset about looking at math problems in a sixth grade math book. She explained that her own mother had helped her realize that she would grow in understanding and be able to do the math problems when she was older.

Beth interrupted the lecture by declaring, "Well, this is a big waste of my time. I could be playing Barbie."

Lectures are useful only when they
don't interfere with a task at hand.

33

Bravery

Lessons of bravery take place throughout life, and we ultimately face challenges with the courage that we develop from the ways we face the trials at the beginning of our lives.

When little Beth's fever had been diagnosed as mono, she faced going to the lab to have her blood drawn. She curled upon her mothers lap, nestling her head on her mother's neck and was so proud that she had not cried. She felt brave and wanted to gloat just a little.

"I am braver than my brother Justin. He cried when he had his tonsils out."

Her mother explained, "According to medical literature researchers think that most children have viruses in a weak form to build up immunity. Now you have increased your immunity and won't get sick so often."

"And I didn't cry," said Beth. "Do I have to take a nap when I'm so brave? Nap is a nasty word."

However after her blood was drawn, she tried not to sleep, but took a nasty nap after all.

It takes a stalwart mother to hold a child
while blood is being drawn.

34

Crèches

Crèches are a wonderful part of our Christmas celebrations. Some crèches are put together on lawns by carpenters. Some crèches are painted by artists. And some crèches have more than a Christmas story to tell. Such is the story of our first crèche.

The story takes place because an editorialist in The Methodist Home advocated that every family should have a crèche for children to use in play. As a dutiful mother of three, I soaked up the advice and traipsed out immediately to find a suitable crèche. It needed to be durable and inexpensive. I headed to the Newberry's store in our new mall. I was in luck. A counter was filled with piles of colorful papier-mâché figures at dime-store prices. The variety was endless. Baby Jesus was crafted with outstretched hands. The manger was a comfy-looking bundle of straw with a recess for the tiny baby. It didn't take long to fill my sack to overflowing with enough crèche figures to keep three children busy.

As I hurried home, I could visualize the Christmas story being reenacted on our family room rug. Teaching the Christmas story with crèche figures was all I hoped it would be. The crèche figures became their favorite toys. The kings and camels marched through the entire house. The angels sang. The animals and shepherds crowded around the manger to see Jesus—or so I thought. One day I realized that Jesus was missing. The manger was there. Mary, Joseph, all the animals and other figures were there, but Jesus was missing. Eagerly the children help me look for Jesus. Despite the fact our house was small, we simply could not find Jesus. We sorted through toys, looked under furniture, and in pockets, but Jesus was gone.

The children quickly resumed their play, happily grouping Mary, Joseph and the shepherds around the empty manger. They babbled contentedly. I felt troubled and lost little time in heading back to Newberry's to get another Baby Jesus. They were pleased to have a baby to put in the manger, and I felt theologically comforted as I watched the children play with the Holy Family.

My comfort didn't last long. In a few days, I realized they had found the lost baby, and they had two babies and two mangers in the cattle stall. Impulsively I announced, "Oh, we can't have two babies. Jesus is God's only son." I reached out to take away one of the mangers. Oh the indignation! The protests! The tears! I took the easy way out and left the babies in the mangers until after everyone went to bed.

Who learned the most from the crèche experience? I thought I did, for I saw a world marching to a manger that was empty— or was it? I was so eager to fill up the manger that I could not wait for someone to find the Christ Child. When I could not find Jesus in the logical places, I gave up. Children accept the fact that Jesus had been with them. That was enough.

May our faith be that of a child who has experienced the presence of Jesus. That is enough. Amen.

Our recollections are ways
of entertaining ourselves throughout life.

Part Two

Sno-Cones

35

Sno-Cones

The adventure began with Teresa's casual remarks before delivering Luke and Eleanor for a grandparent visit, "Oh, by the way, we are sending along their new Sno-Cone maker. They would like to try it out in your neighborhood where the profits might prove more substantial than in our subdivision."

Before I could counter with, "Oh, but we are on a dead-end street," their basket of clothes with the Sno-Cone maker bouncing on top was hefted into our waiting van. We were on the way to Columbia, Missouri, from the rendezvous point near Kansas City.

The excited barrage of questions began, "Neanie, do you have any Kool-Aid that we can put on our Sno-Cones? We need several different kinds. Do you have paper cups and spoons, or maybe straws? Oh, and we need something to make signs out of."

I realized that this would be more than a lemonade stand under a tree. It would be a long orchestrated production.

"No, I do not have any Kool-Aid, but I can get some if we cannot improvise. Yes, I have paper cups and spoons. Yes, I have magic markers and paper for signs." It was time to change the subject. We resorted to riddles and knock-knock jokes to avoid the proverbial, "Are we there yet?"

We arrived in the dark at the house on Cedar Lake and promptly marched off to bed, so we could start the next day early and dig out all the toys that were squirreled away since the last visit from grandchildren. The talking-doll created a scene and had to go sleep with Pa because it insisted on talking and keeping everyone awake. Giggles soon abated, and all were asleep, including the doll.

The next day began with an excited voice calling from the pantry at 6:30 a.m., "Oh, Neanie, we can use Jello for the Sno-Cones. You have all kinds."

"Yes," I acquiesced and insisted that four boxes were enough. We started the stash for the adventure: four boxes of Jello, plastic cups, spoons, straws, Pa's electric cord, a cup of change, a card table, chairs, signs, and a bucket of ice.

I soon learned that the price of 25¢ was non-negotiable. According to Luke's persuasive voice, "We have already discussed the price of 25¢ and have set a reasonable amount to make a profit but not be too much to be discouraging." I realized that a discussion was useless. So it was that we made the signs: "Refreshing Sno-Cones, 25¢." Ellie was quite pleased with the terms and promptly started decorating the signs with what she called her "measles dots."

We were ready, but the neighborhood was not. All were busy in the work-a-day world. We opted to play and swim and wait to set up shop until in the afternoon when the workers came home, and the walkers were on the schedule of exercising their pets. Cousin Beth was happy to join Luke and Ellie in the set-up scene under the red-bud tree in the front yard. Out came the tables, chairs, and signs. Out came the Sno-Cone machine and the syrups. Last, out came the cups, straws, spoons, and a bucket of ice. We were in business, or so I thought.

Then it was that five-year old Ellie grabbed a sign and said, "We have to get people. We need to get customers."

No one was in sight. Garage doors were shut tight. Windows were closed while air-conditioners hummed away. Ellie was undaunted. She ran down the street yelling at the top of her lungs, "Refreshing Sno-Cones, only 25¢." Luke soon joined the clamor and their voices rang shrilly throughout the quiet neighborhood on the dead-end street.

Cousin Beth with fourth grade dignity sat alone at the table and waited with folded arms. Soon Ellie reported back that she had found a man going into his house after work who said he would come and get a snow-cone. Then Ellie proceeded to hop on a bicycle with training wheels and travel a block in the opposite direction calling at the top of her lungs, "Refreshing, tasty Sno-Cones, only 25¢." She made a second round of the cul-de-sac in time to greet the arrival of the neighbors across the street who promised to buy a cone.

The production line was put into action. The ice cubes were fed into the machine and out splattered crunchy ice. The choice of syrups was mixed—with enthusiasm—blueberry, lime, and strawberry. Everyone was happy to be in business. The product was tested using the mixture of syrups and given high approval by the production crew.

Two walkers strolled by and were greeted with the rousing calls for "tasty Sno-Cones, only 25¢." One of the walkers stopped to apologize, and explained that walkers do not carry money. "That's all right" volunteered Ellie. "You can go back and get some."

They smiled and continued their walk. Half an hour later a white truck pulled to the curb. The walker had returned! She sorted out her change to purchase a Sno-Cone and gave coins to all the vendors.

A boy walking a dog pretended not to hear the clarion call, and marched purposefully down the street avoiding eye contact. Three sets of eyes wistfully followed his progress until he was out of sight. Our newspaper girl came by with a paper, and was quite pleased when offered a Sno-Cone since "she had given us a paper." Ellie could not help adding, "We will give you a Sno-Cone, even though we are charging everyone else 25¢." After the newspaper girl finished her paper route, she returned to collect a Sno-Cone and left sauntering down the street slurping a strawberry cone.

Another round of tasting left the supply of ice and syrup rather depleted. The vendors decided that riding bicycles and climbing trees was far more fun and left the stand deserted.

New adventures involve
new learning experiences.

36

Looking for More

Ellie, soon to be two years old, pranced into the kitchen and showed her mother her elbow.

Teresa dutifully admired her elbow, and assured her, "That is your elbow."

Then it was that Ellie crooked her other arm in different positions and announced, "More elbow. More elbow!" Then she picked up a toy spatula and asked, "What's dis?"

"A spatula," her mother answered, and explained by helping Ellie feel the cutting edge. Cautiously Ellie felt the serrated edge of the pie-shaped toy. Slowly Ellie turned the spatula over to rub its back. With volume, she announced, "More spatula, Mama. More spatula."

We laugh at a child appreciating a spatula as an extension of "more" possibilities, and rejoice that in crooked elbows she can recognize the wonder of "more."

Do we miss out on experiences
when we don't look for "more"?

37

Sorting Out Meanings

Justin's cry: "Laa, laa, laah; laa, laa, laah.": *(I'm here. Don't forget me.)*

~~~

Beth: Sniffing her nose and bopping her mouth: *(Put me in my high chair.)*

~~~

Ellie: Soft sigh: *(Well, this is the world I must adjust to now.)*

~~~

Zora: Flop, flop, flop her hands and pinch a nose: *(Wake up. I need attention.)*

~~~

Justin calling his mother: *(Hurry up, Doodle Bug.)*

~~~

Justin's word for yes: *(Yips.)*

~~~

Mother to Justin, "Say thank you.": *(Thank me.)*

~~~

Opening and closing a dishwasher: *(Raise up. Raise down. Raise up. Raise down.)*

~~~

Dough left in the mixing bowl: *(Bonus)*

~~~

Make-up: *(Cereal on Beth's face)*

Language takes practice
and affirmation.

45

38

Secrets

We went bowling and out to eat on Pa's birthday.

Beth got around and whispered to Pa, "We got you two shirts and a pair of pants for your birthday, but you are supposed to be surprise-ed."

That was too good to keep. When Pa told her mother, she questioned Beth, "Why did you tell Pa what his gifts were?"

Beth explained the situation in plain terms, "Because he didn't know."

Good reasoning! The gift in Beth's favorite color consisted of yellow boxer shorts with smiley faces and a yellow sweat shirt with a smiley face and red lips—most appropriate for fishing.

Keeping secrets is an art
that takes practice.

39

Cleaning

When Nanny Judy tried to take the mop away from Justin, so she could finish mopping, he informed her, "Let go, Honey. It's my turn."

Later he got the broom and stashed it away under the couch and explained, "Now I will know where it is when I need it."

~~~

Surely there is nothing better than getting out the vacuum cleaner and finding things to clean with the various attachments.

~~~

To clean the bathroom with a rag and a spray bottle of water is an hour's worth of entertainment, but even more fun is finding a full bottle of Windex. You can be sure the Windex bottle is always empty when it is returned.

For a beginner, the magic of cleaning lies in the numerous cleaning tools and solutions.

40

Hide and Seek

"Let's play hide and seek. You be 'it' first, Neanie. Hide your eyes and count to fifty."

Dutifully, I hid my eyes and counted slowly and loudly to fifty. The grandchildren's game was set on go. Four little bodies scurried to hide in my basement behind furniture, under beds, and in closets.

"Ready or not, here I come."

We took turns being 'it.'

Three-year old Ellie hid in the same place every time and launched a gale of giggles every time we found her in the same place.

Finally, I hid behind the shower curtain in the basement bathroom and waited and waited. Then, I realized the game was going on upstairs without me. I wasn't even missed!

When by-passed in the game of life,
we must find other games to play.

41

Scissors

This week Beth had a scissors education. First she practiced her scissor skills on new clothes that she had never worn and suffered through a lecture on the acceptable uses of scissors.

Then she learned that although scissors were useful tools in cutting hair, they must be used in appropriate places.

Angel had barely escaped a scissors treatment when she was napping after a post-call day at the hospital. Beth begged to play Barbie doll on the king-size bed beside her. All went well. Beth groomed her Barbie doll's head and worked with a box of bows, ribbons, and barrettes beside her mother.

Angel was aroused from her nap by a sound that she couldn't identify, and rolled over to find Beth poised with scissors, ready to tackle her mother's head of thick hair rather than the Barbie Doll's head.

Beth suffered through another lecture on the uses of scissors.

Learning to use tools appropriately
is a lesson all must learn.

42

Halloween

Luke called to inform us that Halloween was coming and that he was going to be a bulldozer and Mama was going to be a backhoe.

When Justin heard the plans, he wanted to know what his Daddy would be? In all seriousness, Luke suggested he could be the dirt. Nothing is more wonderful than dirt, unless it is spray paint or glue.

According to Teresa, making a bulldozer costume out of a cardboard box with spray paint and a glue gun was almost more excitement than Luke could stand—a whole week before Halloween.

~~~

The next Halloween, Teresa called and requested help in making Halloween costumes for her three children. Luke and Ellie wanted to be Venus fly traps with Zora as the fly.

We worked to cut the bottoms out of big, plastic flower pots and wore them with shoulder suspenders. Hands were covered with elbow-length gloves made to look like leaves with red teeth. No energy was left to make Zora's costume. She was just a plain black fly.

~~~

Our house on Cedar Lake adapted to various Halloweens over the years. Usually the order was for furry creatures.

One year Halloween and Homecoming became a joint affair

with everyone becoming a yellow-striped Mizzou tiger with furry ears and a wonderful tails that could be used to spin and hit other Halloween creatures.

The wombat called for the most research, but the thick, fuzzy fur pleased and delighted Luke's creative sensitivity. It was wonderful relief to have Ellie and Zora opt to be just plain witches.

Halloween captures every
child's creative instincts.

43

Accidents

A puppy joined the grandchildren's household, a most contaminating force, but a perfect love gift for children.

After much discussion, the golden retriever puppy inherited the name Airbud. His antics kept everyone entertained. His awkwardness made everything he did ever so cute.

One day while Angel was on call and Justin was at school, I went over to play with Beth and Airbud. In one of our battles, Airbud nipped my finger and made it bleed. Beth flew to the bathroom and got a band-aid (one of her specialties), unwrapped it quickly, and proceeded to put it on my finger quite adroitly. Then she asked with such concern, "Do you think Pa will be mad at you?"

I assured her that it was an accident, and everyone learns to accept accidents without anger.

Accidents serve as reminders to understanding
that things can go wrong.

44

The Red Heart

On a visit to baby-sit three-year-old Luke, I noticed a heart drawn on the back of his hand with a red ball-point pen. Although a bit unsymmetrical, it was perfect enough for me to know that Luke had not drawn it. So I asked him, "Luke, why do you have a red heart drawn on your hand?"

"Oh," Luke informed me rather matter-of-factly, "that's because my daddy loves me." Luke was much too busy playing to offer further comment.

Quickly my daughter stepped in to explain. "Luke gets upset when he wakes up in the morning and finds that his Dad has left early for work without telling him good-by, so Brian reminds him that he has kissed him by drawing a heart on his sleeping hand. When Luke sees the heart on his hand, he knows that his Dad has touched him with love."

***If only we could draw hearts
on all people who need to be touched by love.***

45

The Lounge Singer

Luke set up a one man band. He backed the vacuum cleaner up to the fireplace and hung some pans on it. Then the electronic keyboard was set on the hearth. Some noise makers went on the hearth opposite the keyboard.

The musical show began. He started the auto-drum and after several beats announced, "Ladies and Gentlemen, I have some very special songs for you to hear. Now clap your hands and sing with me."

He started banging the pots and pans with a plastic golf club to establish a beat. The noise of the beat was taken over by the noisemakers, and music was played on the keyboard in a medley of locomotive songs which he sang, first "Dinah Blow Your Horn," then "Down by the Station," and last "New River Train."

All he needed to add was a few lame jokes, and he could have been rented out to the local Ramada Inn.

***Improvisation is a useful
musical form to learn.***

46

Plastic Grocery Sacks

Ellie collects tags from plastic grocery sacks, carries them around the house and plays with them.

Once she took a nap with a tag. When her mother picked her up, she retrieved the tag before she would lift her hands to be taken from her bed. When her mother inadvertently sat on a tag, Ellie proclaimed loudly, "You are sitting on my tag. Hurry, get up!"

When she retrieved the tag, she cooed to it in a loving voice, "Oh, little tag, little tag."

We learn what people treasure
and abide by their peculiarities.

47

Baths

Oh, how Beth loves baths!

One morning she heard Angel taking a bath before going to work at 5:00 a.m. She proceeded to dash in the bath room and slither into the tub of water.

Her mother scatted her out with, "No, it is too early. You get back in bed."

She left with her wet body wrapped in her "ni-ni" and slowly crawled back into her bed.

Baths are wonderful entertainment
until you _have_ to take them.

48

Tooth Stories

While we were brushing our teeth before bedtime, Beth watched me ever so closely. Finally she stopped and quizzed me, "Neanie, can you take out your teeth?"

I laughed and assured her, "No, of course not."

"Well, Pa can," she retorted with such delight. His partial plate fascinated her.

~~~

We got a phone call from Luke. "Hello, Neanie, I have a loose tooth. I really do."

"Oh, that is wonderful," I responded.

"Well, Dad is in Chicago and won't come home until after tomorrow, and I just had to tell someone, so I called you."

~~~

I was visiting at Zora's house when she lost a tooth. She had worked at it for several days and finally managed to get it out. Everyone admired it, and waited for Mama and Ellie to get home from an errand so they could see it.

Suddenly we heard a piercing cry from the bathroom. We ran to see what had happened. Zora had dropped the tooth in the sink, and it had rolled into the drain.

What a tragedy! Would the tooth fairy come if the tooth were lost? Zora was inconsolable. I assured her I would try to get it out. No such luck with the drain.

When her Mama and Ellie came home, we shared our sad story. Ellie went to work on the drain, and soon appeared with a tooth. All tears were dried.

That evening the door bell rang, and the Tooth Fairy appeared in crazy garb and delivered money for a tooth.

*The pain of loosing a tooth is
minimized by the wonderful Tooth Fairy.*

49

Morning Litany

"Hey, Mommy and Daddy, the sun is up. That means it is time to get up and make pancakes. Get up. Get up—just look. The sun is up. It's all bright outside and getting warm. We should all get up and eat something together. I like to get up when the sun gets up. The sun heats me up, and then I eat breakfast. Just like that. I can't wait FOREVER. The sun is up and I NEED to get up now and EAT SOME PANCAKES. I'd like syrup on those pancakes. I'd probably like some sprinkles too. Neanie gives me sprinkles. They are so funny and tasty too. That would be very fun."

The monologue does not cease until someone picks Luke up.

Morning is a joy when the sun
wakes the world—and children.

50

Swimming Lessons

Arrangements were made for Justin and Beth to take swimming lessons so they would be safe at their Grandparents' home on Cedar Lake. They went happily to the pool for the lesson.

Beth took one look at the teacher and whispered to me, "She's big like a witch. Please get in the water with me."

"Do you want me to get in, clothes and all?" I asked. I opted to sit on a stool by the water's edge.

Soon Beth learned that the teacher closed each lesson by having them jump off the diving board. What fun! Then Beth was eager to cut each lesson short so she could jump more.

Finally, she decided it would be easier if she just took jumping lessons and by-passed the tedious swimming routine. "Can I take jumping, lessons, Mom?"

Lessons of all kinds
help us build new skills.

51

When One Can Read

On Wednesdays Luke's dad would go to preschool to have lunch with Luke. His friends thought that this was really neat.

One day, one of Luke's playmates asked his Dad, "Luke's Daddy, can you read?"

As soon as Brian reported that he could indeed read, he was engulfed by four little boys piling on his lap, each with a book.

We learn early the pleasure
that is wrapped up in reading.

52

Philosophical Insights

Teresa prods Luke to think values.

"If you were a father what do you think would be the most important thing to teach your children?

"Well, I guess love—love would be the most important. And, then I think fighting. It is important not to fight and kill. And then I think, don't mix all your paints together or you will just get a brown blob."

Practical insights are as important
as philosophical ones.

53

Dinosaurs

Every little boy is fascinated by dinosaurs. There are multiple books on every level, preschool through elementary, with pictures of dinosaurs tromping through jungles and fighting with other dinosaurs. There are little dinosaurs, massive dinosaurs, flying dinosaurs, and crawling dinosaurs.

Justin came to our house for a visit, bringing his often read dinosaur books. My duty, as a grandmother, was to read to him. That I did, but after I got weary, I shortened the text on one. After I finished it, I was dutifully reminded that the author says, "This one eats low growing plants."

Woe unto me! I had omitted a fact that the writer had included. I couldn't believe a three-year old could not be duped into a shorter version of the book.

We must be diligent in recounting <u>all</u> facts
about plant-eating dinosaurs to little children!

54

Card Makers

When I had a knee replacement, first grader Beth came flying into the house with cards she had made for me to bolster my recovery. One featured a scotch-taped, bounce-out insert that said, "I love you, Neanie."

Scotch tape was a Beth specialty. The card that melted me was one which included words from her Dick and Jane Reader: "Go, go, go Neanie. Run, run, run." Cards would surely help me be able to run soon.

~~~

Justin made me a get-well card on the computer. He carefully hunted down the keyboard letters of the message he had his mother write for him. He thought that I could read the printing better than his writing. I think I probably could have if he had let me open the card, but he was so proud of it, he couldn't bear to put it in my hands. Along with the computer card he brought a picture of a horse that he had colored in multi-colored stripes because he just knew I would want to see it.

~~~

At school, Beth made a Mother's Day card for her mother. In the card, she thanked her mother for playing with her, and decorated it with a white feather. When she turned it in to her teacher, she reported, "Mothers really do like cards. They put them up and keep them so they can remember their children in case they die."

Cards lift our spirits, especially
hand-made ones, if we get to see them.

55

The Educational Garden

We set out to entertain our grandchildren with an educational garden. We planted a variety of seeds in the bed in our backyard, landscaped with railroad ties and located on the walkway to our dock at the lake.

First, we had a lesson on earthworms which the children initially refused to touch, but Pa's enthusiasm for using worms as fishing bait encouraged them to join in collecting mama worms, daddy worms, and baby worms.

Then we went through tasting onion blades, lettuce, and spinach leaves. Beth learned her lesson well and was later found tasting house plants in their sun room when she went home, telling her mother they were "onyons."

Luke saw the young cattails by the boat dock and excitedly called out, "Oh, look everyone. There are "onyons" in the lake. My onion lesson didn't get off to the best start.

Next, I turned to potatoes. I was sure they would be thrilled to see the baby potatoes, but Justin deflated my ego by informing me, "Grandpa Cleo has a bigger garden with a long row of potatoes. I helped him dig them last week."

I tried making zucchini bread with their help. At least I had plenty of zucchini, anything to use up the squash. They did enjoy the bread, somewhat, but were more interested in playing with the dough.

Happy was Beth when she pulled up a bunch of green tops and was thrilled to find a carrot on the end of them. She later found that a combination of tomatoes and strawberries was truly delectable.

Learning about food through a beginner's garden can be an inventive source for new recipes.

56

Vocabulary

Luke has wonderful fun with vocabulary.

Teresa took him to a grocery story that gave children cookies while their parents shopped, quite a treat for Luke. Luke took the cookie in his hand and cooed, "Oh, mama, just look at this cookie. It makes me so embarrassed."

Teresa could never convince him that embarrassed was not the right word. How does one go about explaining embarrassment to a two-year old?

When they were traveling through down-town Kansas City, Luke commented, "Oh, mama, look at the tall buildings. They are ice scrapers." No convincing him otherwise.

"Now, Mom, I don't think Darth Vader is such a bad guy. He just makes poor choices."

If you say so!

All our lives we discover new words
and have fun figuring out ways to use them.

57

Christmas Eve

The family Christmas Eve service at our church calls for all children to participate and come dressed as shepherds, angels, or kings. The youngest baby in the congregation gets to be the Baby Jesus.

My sewing machine was put to good use, and we contrived to create appropriate costumes.

Alas, Beth refused to wear a dowdy, brown shepherd's robe when she had a shimmery princess play-dress. It is not easy to argue effectively with a two-year old. Her mother saved the situation by calling her a "king," and she stood at the manger with the Wise Men, ever so pleased.

~~~

The next year we opted to dress her as an angel with coat-hanger wings, covered elegantly with lace. She could flutter down the isle with all the other fluttering angels who kept adjusting their haloes and take her place beside the baby, who cried.

Justin was a regal king who marched all the way from the back of the church with two adult kings who served as ushers. His crown was magnificent. No one could possibly guess that it was a green bean can sprayed gold and bedecked with jewels, and that a perfectly good place mat had also been sprayed gold to serve as the collar for his purple robe. It was serious business bringing gifts to the Christ Child with the wise men from afar who stood so solemnly by the Baby Jesus.

~~~

When Luke and Ellie came at Christmas, they joined the pageant and all became angels, kings or shepherds.

Participating as angels, wise-men, and shepherds help children remember the Christmas story.

58

Three Games

After school I was elected to play games, first by Justin. We played Sony Play Station. Justin kept shouting orders about what I must do, mainly, "You're going the wrong way, Neanie."

At my left, Beth had her Barbies and a doll trailer with a sink that spouted running water. She insisted that I be the doll with the long white hair.

Meanwhile Airbud, the dog, nosed in and licked me if I didn't throw a ball down the hall for him to chase.

Learning to juggle various activities at the same time teaches parents to be flexible.

Demands on our time
keep life exciting.

59

Obeying Mother

Weddings are tedious affairs when you are a flower girl and your brother is the ring bearer. Waiting is not easy for a two-year old in a new dress, but Ellie managed the ceremony with no glitches and felt a freedom in the procession out of the church into the open air.

The bright sun made the outdoor water fountain look exciting beyond words. Happily she burst forth, "Now can I go play in the fountain?"

Her mother's voice was firm but forceful, "Not yet. You wait right where you are." And wait she did. However, when her mother realized the guests were waiting patiently to exit the chapel, did she see a woman frantically mouthing words, "Your microphone is still on. Your microphone is still on."

Dutifully the guests who arose to follow the procession out of the chapel, sat back down when they heard an amplified voice admonish them, "Not yet. You wait right where you are."

The importance of our mother's voice
resounds all through our lives.

Part Three

Dragons
and
Such

60

The Magic Dragon

We were a captive audience! Two-year-old Luke had learned a new song that he wanted to sing for us. He had a play-microphone ready for the rendition. His Dad was ready at the piano and led with a stirring introduction. Luke bounced to the rhythm on the step beside the baby grand piano and launched forth into the chorus of "Puff, the Magic Dragon lived by the sea and 'pottied' in the autumn mist in a land called Honah Lea."

I caught my breath and listened carefully as he repeated the lines of the chorus the second time. "Puff, the Magic Dragon lived by the sea and 'pottied' in the autumn mist." There it was again. He had substituted "pottied" for "frolicked," a word much more familiar to a two-year-old than the word "frolic." Perhaps a dragon would find it more comfortable to potty in the thick mist, if indeed a Magic Dragon needed to potty.

We read into our songs
the experiences we have encountered.

61

Swinging

It started out with a four foot swing attached under the balcony of the deck to our house that offered a view of Cedar Lake to the swingers.

While swinging, we watched the geese coast in, splattering the water as they landed, honking greetings to all their friends. We found the jostling motion of a swing comforting to the pushers and the riders, to babies and adults, and to talkers and lookers.

Soon the clamor of grandchildren took over. "I want a swing I can push with my feet."

Pa's wood working skills were called into play. He built a horse and a cow and hung them as glider swings on either side of the big swing. The heads of the animals on a horizontal board sailed through the air, and the tails swished in the wind. Rain soon washed off the eyes glued on the horse, but lasted longer than the rubber glove glued on as an udder for the cow.

Next a ladder was added from the ground to the balcony with a rope knotted and suspended so that children could climb the ladder, grab the rope, and swing out to jump on a mat on the lawn. The finishing touches were a round disc threaded on a rope that could be mounted by sitters or standers and a fireman's tube to help the descent from the ladder go faster. The cries of animals, trains and engines supplied the sounds that made the swings go higher.

Swings catch the imagination
of children of all ages.

62

The Montessori Way

As an observer, my eyes took in the large room filled with toys in boxes of all shapes, sizes, and materials. Children looked for something they wished to play with, and all soon found a toy. When one child dropped his box of toy parts, I jumped up to help him pick up the pieces. The teacher immediately stopped me and told me forcefully that it was the child's responsibility, his "work." I was to be patient and praise him for picking up the toy. I was allowed to admire the tasks they were completing and listen to children discuss the wonder of their work. I finally got the hang of the class.

When it was time to go home, we went to the cloak room, and I watched as they put on their coats, mittens and hats—what a riot! I did not think I could sit still and watch them attempt to put arms in sleeves backwards, but I did. Luke put on his coat upside down. He made several attempts in different directions and finally got one hand in a sleeve and then another hand, grabbed the tail of the coat and pulled it up around his face looking ever so pleased. He had done his work. The teacher praised him and suggested that maybe she could turn it around for him so he could get it buttoned. He didn't know she took the coat completely off him and together they buttoned it.

Still, I will never forget the pleased smile that erupted after he got the coat on upside down.

Accomplishing new tasks
always gives us a thrill.

63

Scabs

Beth went to the podiatrist to have a wart checked that had been removed from the bottom of her foot. Beth intended to show the doctor her carefully salvaged wart scab, which she had originally kept in a glass box until her mother prevailed on her to put it into a zip-lock bag.

I got a frantic phone call from Beth at the doctor's office, "Please, Neanie, can you go by my house and get the plastic bag I left on the kitchen counter with the wart scab so I can show it to the doctor?" By all means! Aren't all grandmothers expected to chase down scabs for show and tell? The doctor acted as thrilled to see a wart scab as Beth had expected and confided that she had two little girls and appreciated how valuable scabs are.

Show-and-tell is always more effective
with an object in hand.

64

Monopoly

While Justin was sick, I entertained him one morning by playing a new version of Monopoly with footballs for dice. When he landed on a $60 team, I asked him if he wanted to buy it. He informed me, "Not for $60. They aren't even worth a $1. They have won only four games all year."

Next year I won't buy a Football Monopoly game and be humiliated by a six-year old because I didn't follow current football teams.

Early in life we learn the
importance of statistics and value.

65

Tea Parties

Is anything more wonderful than planning a tea party? First we round up all the guests—dolls and stuffed animals—and seat them at a table. Then we add place cards with proper scribbles. We hunt down all the best china with cups, saucers, plates and a tea pot. It doesn't matter whether the "china" matches or not. Oh yes, a sugar bowl and a cream pitcher are vitally essential.

Now we are ready for a feast with Beth, Ellie and Zora. We take whatever cookies or crackers we can find, and then fill up the tea pot with water. The tiny cups of water turn immediately into delicious tea.

A tea set is invaluable
in teaching culinary arts.

66

The New Baby

Nothing is more wonderful than going to the hospital to see a new baby, especially when it is your baby sister.

The morning after Beth's birth, Justin was primed to go and see his new sister at the hospital. In fact, Justin had been ready for some time. He danced around the house swinging a basket and waiting for visiting hours. At last it was time to get in the car.

Justin ran and salvaged his Easter basket. We suggested he leave it at home. "No," he said, "I need to take it with me."

When we got to the hospital, he grabbed the basket, bounced into the hospital, and said, "You see, I will need something to bring the baby home in."

He forgot about the basket when he saw how big Baby Beth was. He sat quietly watching her and went into gales of laughter when she flexed her toes. He brought home the empty basket.

It is always rewarding to watch a new baby,
even one too big for an Easter basket.

67

Learning to be Big

Our task was to babysit three year old Luke when Ellie, his sister, was born. We came prepared. The biggest hit was Pa's tools for putting up curtain rods, particularly a drill. Luke found the sewing machine equally entertaining. He had to learn the joy of being helpful and big. It wasn't always easy.

One evening he told his mother, "I wish we could close all the doors and tell every body to leave. Then do you think you could sit beside me and read just one book?"

Mission accomplished.

Parents learn that acclimating to
a new child in the family takes time.

68

Landscaping

Justin paraded through their new house that was being built on a hill and checked out all the things the carpenters were using.

The array of paint cans lined up in the hall was intriguing, but the sawdust and wood shavings by the front door were the most enticing attraction.

The next trip to the new house, Justin scouted up a battery of toys and brought them along. He was ready to work with the carpenters using a dump truck, a grader, a back-hoe, a bull-dozer, a hammer and an assortment of toy shovels. Each trip to the new house he brought more toys to "work" on the pile of wood shavings by the front door.

One morning a carpenter walked by and suggested that Justin was getting more accomplished outside than they were inside.

We learn patterns of industry
by watching others at work.

69

Snow Angels

It was the first snow of the season and brought a measure of excitement that only a child can experience. I got a call from Angel, "Mother, can we come over to your house? You have a better yard for playing on our sleds."

Nothing is more fun than playing with children in a new snow.

"Of course," I said. Soon they were tromping in their little red boots through the three inch snow.

Beth's mother shared her daughter's newly acquired wisdom. "Beth has learned that making snow angels on your stomach does not work as well as making snow angels on your back."

Learning from our mistakes
is a lesson we seldom forget.

70

How to Play Barbies

This week I learned how to play Barbies. Don't laugh! Seven-year-old Beth informed me, "You don't know how to play Barbies, Neanie. You always just dress them up."

I laughed because I realized that my first impulse, indeed, was to dress the naked Barbies with twisted legs, ratted hair, and bare busts writhing in a basket of Barbie clothes.

Angel had relegated the mess and mass to their unfinished basement on an area rug. Along with the Barbies went the dollhouse, the stable, horses, the Barbie car, a camper, and a shopping mall. "Playing Barbies" meant more than dressing the dolls in appropriate attire.

Beth explained, "You must talk to the Barbies, direct them to take riding lessons, swim, sign up for soccer lessons, join the children on the playground or shop in the mall."

I became quite good at fabricating conversations, so much so that I got an invitation to come back the next day and play Barbies again. Perhaps I should not have tried so hard to be entertaining.

Tuning into pretend play
stretches our imaginations.

71

Tasting

I got an important phone call from Angel that went something like this, "Guess what Mr. Adorable did this morning! Justin insisted on eating spoonfuls of 'tup' (catsup) with his cereal."

He, at one and a half years had just finished supervising cookie-making and had tasted all the ingredients—flour, soda, salt, sugar, and oil, before he got to the chocolate chips and nuts.

Exploring tastes gives
a new dimension to our lives.

72

Playing Stories

"I know what we can play," said Justin with enthusiasm. "I will be the 'Icked Itch' and you can be a 'Hi-ho.'"

"What's a Hi-ho?" I asked.

"Oh, don't you know? There are seven of them. They help Snow White work."

So I marched around the basement singing, "Hi-ho, hi-ho, it's off to work we go."

Soon Justin joined me, because it looked like more fun marching and singing than being a wicked witch. We dug with shovels, walked over the couch mountain, and marched through a pretend stream of water in the bathtub, all the while singing "Hi-ho, hi-ho, it's off to work we go."

Stretching our imaginations
opens doors to new ideas.

73

Car in the Hole

The most exciting adventure happened when Justin's nanny, Judy Ebdon, took him to a music class for toddlers. The parking lot was crowded, so Judy parked on a plywood board, which unbeknownst to her, was covering a hole.

All went well, until Justin finished his class, came out and got in the car. When Judy pulled away, the board broke, and Judy's car sank into the large hole, so large that a tow truck had to be called to get the car out.

That was just more excitement than Justin could stand in one day. He came home and asked Judy to tell the story over and over, and his mother to tell the story over and over, and he vowed he would be a tow truck driver when he grew up.

They even made up a song about "Miss Judy's car fell in a hole, in a hole, in a hole" and played a newly invented game, *Car in the Hole,* with boards, trucks and holes all summer.

***Out of adversity we learn to adapt
to new experiences with creativity.***

74

Santa Claus

Luke came sauntering into the house and informed his mother, "I've just been outside looking, and I've done some comparing. Santa will not fit into the chimneys on our street. We need to tell everyone to leave their doors open."

*Comparing is a vital skill
to cultivate.*

75

Rules, Rules!

Absorbing rules that come with kindergarten is the most difficult part of adjusting—when to hold hands, how to put toys away and when to throw things.

Luke was set against the "hold-the-hand-of-your-buddy" system to get children to and from the playground. Mostly he wanted to hop and skip around and soak up everything.

Why would anyone want to put toys away in a box when they would want to play with them after they came back from recess? And why would anyone go outside and be told not to throw things on the playground? Where could he throw things? There was no more perfect place than on a playground!

**Rules are sometimes
very difficult to understand.**

76

Fishing Stories

When your grandparents live on a lake, fishing stories abound. First you learn that Pa keeps lures and plastic worms under his boat seat.

Worms are about as good as you can get when their innovative character takes over in a bathtub. Pa doles out a plastic worm to each grandchild and sends them to the house to take a bath with the worms. Off the children go to fill the bathtubs. The colored worms swim over the soap and under the bubbles. They hide in the toys and climb on the back of the rubber frog. They slither under wet bodies and in wet hair. The fun is endless. The bathtub is a mess of mashed, colored worms.

When Pa and Zora go fishing, Pa hooks the fish and lets Zora reel them in. What fun! They caught eight fish. Pa asks, "Do you know you caught eight fish?"

"Really?" Zora answers, "Luke and Ellie will never believe me."

"I'll tell them," Pa assures her.

Zora responds quickly, "Oh, Pa, they will never believe you. No one believes you." She knew Pa teased everyone, and they had trouble telling what was true and what was not.

All that aside, the best part of a fishing trip was to count the fish and release a tub of them one by one to swim away happily in the lake.

Fishermen are loved by all
—even Jesus.

77

Do Unto Others

Luke, when caught doing something obnoxious to Eleanor, was sent to his room. He slammed the door.

When confronted, he informed his mother, "Listen, you are not even doing like Jesus who said, 'Do unto others.' Jesus knew to be a good person you must teach respectfully."

Teresa informed him that he needed to come up with some strategies to take the place of the door slamming. He was no longer unhappy.

He had something to think about.

Working out strategies
to solve problems is a satisfying labor.

78

Cookie Making

Surely making cookies with a grandchild is a cook's joy. However, Beth took time out from cooking to give me some instructions, exploding with, "Neanie, you can find more things to do. Cleaning up a kitchen is not nearly as much fun as messing it up."

"Well, Beth," I answered thoughtfully, "I think that butter wrappers and egg shells really need to go in the trash can. Perhaps we need to move the trash can under the table, since that is where all your mess seems to land."

Learning to be orderly
is not always fun.

79

The Play Kitchen

Beth received a wonderful gift—a play-kitchen. It even had a reservoir for water in the play sink and a faucet that could be turned on to fill cups and glasses. At times she would play pretend with the kitchen sink, but the more exciting thing was to use real water.

On an evening while her mother was on call at the hospital, Beth ask her father for water to play with in the sink. He suggested that she just play pretend with it.

It started off as pretend, but soon Beth became resourceful and went into the bath room. By making several trips with a cup, she was able to fill up the reservoir of her sink with water from the toilet. It was a perfect solution. No one was any the wiser, at least for a while.

Innovative solutions to problems
can always be found.

80

Chandelier Climbing

As soon as a child can crawl, the exploration urge prompts more venturesome feats.

Beth's agility prompted her to attempt more feats than were healthy. She saw the delightful chandeliers hanging in her house, the big one in the foyer and the smaller one over the kitchen table. The lights fascinated her.

A mountain climbing venture was born. First she hiked herself up by squirming up onto a kitchen chair. From there she managed to mount the table. On the table was a flower pot with a plant. She climbed up the flower pot and found she could reach the chandelier. That's when her mother turned around and found her dangling from a chandelier. Enough climbing!

Beware! The exploration instinct
develops at an early age.

81

The New Hair Cut

The new hair cut did not please Beth. She looked in one mirror and did not like what she saw. She tried another mirror and complained about the way she looked.

Her mother comforted her by saying, "Oh, your hair will grow out again soon, and you can get another haircut."

She tried two other mirrors. They confirmed what the first two showed. Then she solved her problem. She would take care of the mirrors. She grabbed a bar of soap and soaped all the mirrors. She would not have to look at herself.

*Solving problems can take on
varieties of experiences.*

82

Coloring Easter Eggs

When Beth first learned about Easter egg dying, it was a magical experience. What could be more wonderful than to dye something besides eggs?

She had an idea. She would go to work on Airbud, her dog. She managed to scrounge up stuff that might serve as a paste to rub on Air bud, and she went to work. She rubbed anything she could find on him. Then she resorted to coloring stripes on him so that he would, indeed, look like an Easter egg.

Airbud did not seem to mind. If fact, he enjoyed the attention until her mother attempted to clean the mess off with soap and water.

Not all techniques work
in new situations.

83

Cousin Grant

Cousin Grant came to study for the C.P.A. exam at the Stewart home. He was intrigued by little Beth who visited one day. When he tried to talk to her, she would hide. He finally gave her a toy. She escaped to the back yard out of sight and came around to the front door to by-pass meeting Grant in the basement.

When asked why she didn't want to see Grant, she explained. "Cause he looks like a giant." Finally Grant played peek-a-boo behind trees, and she learned to like all six feet four inches of him.

First impressions of people
are often misleading.

84

The Art of Singing

Children's choir was a new experience for Justin. He was happy to sing in the choir room, but when it came to lining up on the steps in the sanctuary of the church and singing for the worshippers, he preferred to watch what was going on in the pews while the other children sang.

Finally his mother took over and promised that she would get him a new toy if he sang so people could hear him. That did it. He shouted out every word so no one could miss hearing him.

When he got home, he got the new toy and a lecture about using his singing voice, not his shouting voice.

Oh, there is so much
to learn about music!

85

Death of a Hamster

Justin and Beth's hamster died. It was a sad day. Then they learned that animals could be embalmed. That sounded like a perfect solution. They could keep the hamster forever.

They found a gorgeous gift bag. They then sprinkled the body with carpet freshener and proceeded to wrap it in colorful wrapping paper. Just to be on the safe side, they dumped the whole container of carpet freshener in the sack before setting it on the mantle of the fireplace.

Mission accomplished.

Embalming is a time honored
and fragrant way to enhance life.

86

Death of Maxwell

Maxwell the cat had lived a long life and was feeling poorly. As the children faced his dying days, they discussed what they could do for their pet.

They could take him to the vet, caress him and let the vet put him to sleep. Then they could bring him home and bury him in the back yard. There was the possibility, however, of putting his ashes in a box and setting him on the coffee table where all could pet his box.

That seemed the perfect solution.

Dealing with death
is never easy.

87

Oh, Harry Potter!

One day when Justin was in first grade, I quizzed him, "what is your favorite subject?"

He quickly answered, "Harry Potter."

Well, who is Harry Potter?" I asked.

"Oh, he is in a book that our teacher got in England and reads to us every day at school before we go home. Oh, Neanie, do you think you could get me a Harry Potter book? They have them in the book store. My friends have them."

What grandmother would refuse to get her grandchild a book? "Yes, I'll go tomorrow."

I took the Harry Potter book and went to class to observe a reading session the last hour of the day. There sat the children around their teacher. Most of them had Harry Potter books. They turned to the page the teacher was reading. They were first graders—they couldn't read the books.

As I watched, I could hear Justin's voice ring out, "Oh, but Neanie, I can hold the book while the teacher reads."

Would that all writers could stir
our imaginations so powerfully.

88

What's Pestering?

Justin came home from school reporting, "Beth chases me at school and kisses me. Will you tell her to stop?"

So in motherly fashion, Beth was dutifully instructed not to chase Justin at school and kiss him.

Beth listened and came up with something better. She could get her friends to chase Justin. That would work.

Next came a lecture on "pestering."

Why do people pester? Do they want to bother a person? What is accomplished by pestering? Can you play chase without pestering? Finally, an ultimatum was given—do not pester Justin at school.

Oh, that all people could judge when
to pester and when not to pester.

89

School Bus Time

Luke watched the children come and go on a school bus. In the morning children would board the bus with lunch pails and books, and in the evening they would come home with papers, books, babbling ideas to each other and chasing each other on the path to their houses. Finally Luke reached a happy conclusion.

"Mama," he announced, "you won't need to take me to Ms. Wanda's house for child care tomorrow. I'll just take the bus, since I am so big now."

Can a two-year-old take
a school bus to child care?

90

Hunting for Answers

"Do you think if we grew a tail out of our tail it would hurt when it broke through?" pondered Luke as he quizzed his mother.

"Oh, I don't think so," Teresa responded.

Luke paused a moment and launched another question, "Don't people know babies are born each day and that millions hit the earth every day?"

Questions open doors
to many possibilities.

91

Singing Without Interruptions

One night when two year old Ellie was restless, she reported that she needed to sing a song.

Her mother asked, "Well, what song?"

Ellie promptly filled her in by cutting short any interrogations. "'Row Your Boat Ashore.' Listen to my words. I mean it. You listen to my words. I talking. You listen to my words."

Working to avert interruptions
is a useful talent—at times.

92

Oh, the Bother of a Coat!

The teacher reported to Teresa that Luke kept his coat on all day. Teresa didn't ask why because she had the story of her brother Don's coat etched in her catalogue of memories.

Don's second grade teacher reported at teacher conference that Don loved his wind-breaker and wore it all day, even on hot days.

"Oh, no," the explanation solved the problem, "He's just like his uncle. He just didn't want to bother to take it off and put it back on."

Many of the tedious problems of the world
can be solved in simple ways.

93

Football Injuries

Luke, after playing football with his older cousin and Pa, reported to his kindergarten class that he had a stiff ankle.

He waited until the class got quiet to listen to him while he explained that it was because he had hurt it playing football.

His teacher respectfully commiserated about Luke's football injury to both him and his mother.

***Injuries are a wonderful way
to gain attention!***

94

Mowing People Down

Luke came home puzzled and asked his mother, "Why did Jay try to mow us down with the ball?"

His mother paused, then answered, "I don't know, but how did that make you feel—good or bad?"

"Good," Luke quickly answered, "because then I could fight him."

Do we <u>have</u> to have
reasons for wars?

95

Art Class

Luke's art teacher came to his class and drew a turtle explaining circles, angles and lines, then commissioned each student to draw a turtle.

Luke sat looking off into space, finally beamed and said, "I know what I'll do. I will draw mountains where turtles live, and I'll draw a box for turtles. Then, I will draw a shuttle cock to knock turtles into traps."

He never had time to draw the turtle.

Blessed are those whose minds reach
beyond the simple art assignment.

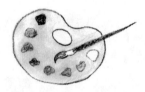

96

Kindergarten Circle

It seems that the morning reading circle at school is known as the important time for exchanging new ideas.

After Luke came home from kindergarten, his mother pumped him for information about what went on in the circle.

Luke said that he was tired and that he would tell her eventually when Dad came home so he wouldn't have to tell it twice.

To avoid duplicating efforts
is a way to simplify life.

97

Hope

All evening Ellie was pensive and quiet, couldn't seem to get involved in playing.

Finally she explained to her mother, "I wish you had not told me that Pa and Neanie might come. I just can't seem to turn my hope off."

According to the Apostle Paul,
we should never turn our hope off.

98

Encounter with a Butterfly

After one of Zora's soccer games, Teresa called to report an interesting happenstance.

It seems that in the middle of soccer game, a butterfly drifted over the cluster of little girls gathered around the ball that they were kicking up and down the soccer field.

Soon a voice rang out, "There's a butterfly!"

The game stopped. Everyone watched the children wheel and follow the fluttering butterfly down the field and away from the ball. Coaches folded their arms, and amused parents watched little hands reach for the alluring butterfly until it drifted out of sight, and the game resumed.

Children remind us to stop and catch
butterfly moments that sensitize our lives.

Part Four

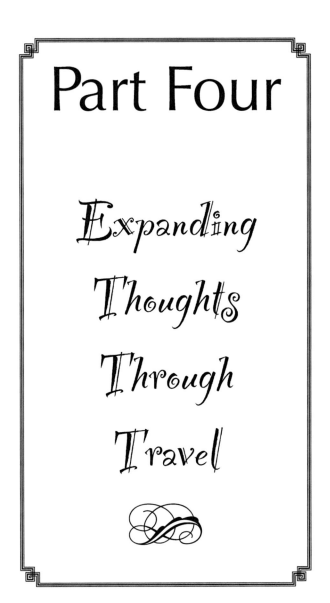

Expanding

Thoughts

Through

Travel

99

Excavating Dinosaur Bones

When Justin and Beth explored Disney World in Florida, they began with a tour of Cinderella's Castle and finished off with an excavation of dinosaur bones embedded in mounds of loose sand. They tackled the excavation of bones with the single mindedness of all great scientists, working under the hot sun. Afterwards, they walked through all the water sprays and drenched their hair to cool off.

Fortunately, Beth did not have to worry about her bangs, for she had cut them off when she decided that "bangs are for goats." Justin was immeasurably pleased when a Moroccan entertained him by writing his name from right to left in Arabic and gave him a copy of his alphabet.

The adults supervised the rides. Early one morning Justin informed me, "Today you can go with me on the Star-Wars ride again, Neanie. You have been on it only once." He then proceeded to give me instructions, "If you get scared, just hold on tight with your hands and the twisty turns and falls won't bother you."

Beth pronounced most emphatically, "I don't EVER want to go on the Star-Wars ride again."

We stayed in Wilderness Lodge, a hotel built by Disney to simulate Yellowstone Park Lodge with a water spray spouting hourly.

Travel challenges our minds
to find new patterns of thought.

100

Off to "Hamaica"

It was our family's first trip together by air to Jamaica. On lift-off, Ellie, Luke and Beth took window seats. Two-year-old Ellie reported first.

Breathlessly she cried out, "Oh, my, we are floating in the sky." For several weeks she had been suggesting that she was ready to go to "Hamaica." Usually her words were, "I have a good idea. Let's go to Hamaica now."

Justin located the new Harry Potter book in the air terminal and carried it as if it were a priceless treasure, actually a "Golden Goblet."

Beth came with face paint so that they could wear Harry Potter scars. I delivered silly-putty, and the playing began. However, the early flight put everyone in napping mode after breakfast. Luke kept himself awake by talking non-stop, and we were soon in Jamaica.

Through the eyes of children
we see the world in a floating perspective.

101

A Goat in My Road

Hungry children made the two-hour driving trip to the Jamaican resort a tedious one.

Everywhere we looked we saw cows tethered—along the roadsides, in church yards, among the tombstones in cemeteries, in city parks and on post-office lawns. There were no lawn mowers, only cows. At one point three goats crossed the road in front of our taxi. I thought surely the taxi driver would slow down.

"No problem," he said as two goats scurried across and one quickly turned back.

We managed to breeze through them with no hesitation.

We can be glad we are not
goats in Jamaica.

102

Cannons and Coral and Crabs, Oh My!

We planned our day and arranged kid-watching shifts after Ellie, who is absolutely fearless, informed her mother, "I would like to do that by myself," pointing to parasailers dangling against the beautiful blue sky in the wind. We ignored her enthusiasm and signed up for snorkeling.

Teresa stayed on the beach and made sand castles with Luke, who had a broken arm. I can still hear Justin calling from the snorkeling area, "Neanie, follow me. Hurry! I have found the ship wreck and canon. It is covered with coral."

I am not sure how Justin's little, thin legs manage to manipulate fins so deftly. He was a pro at diving down with his mask and surfacing to blow out the salt water. Later in the week he came up with a baby starfish and managed to catch a tiny fish with a piece of nylon net. Beth did not like the salt water in her eyes but swam like a porpoise in the resort pool.

The children found nothing more entertaining than the crabs. They came in all sizes from eight-inch dark ones to the small ghost crabs that skittered sideways on the beach. The children giggled and shrieked as they chased crabs or sought to avoid them. Each night, a flash-light hunt for crabs brought new prospects. Beth had the local crab holes around her cabin numbered for surveillance. Crabs on the beach could be dug up or flushed out with water. One day they found a baby crab. What ecstasy!

To someone from a land-locked state,
nothing is more wonderful than an ocean beach.

103

Flashlight Hunts

On the beach for the Sabbath, we sang "This is the Day the Lord Hath Made" and shared sacred thoughts. The children patted sand into shapes while they set up a "Sandbox Church." Beth told the story of the plague of frogs in Egypt. The picture in the Bible Storybook showing Pharaoh's marble palace littered with green frogs fascinated Beth. The beach was a perfect place to share the story.

On one flashlight hunt, we looked for the noisy tree frogs. We even speculated that the resort was simulating their peeping because it sounded so electronic—a touch of ambiance. Surely there were five thousand! Then we found a frog, no bigger than the end of a thumb, sounding off with a shrill peeping that pierced the night air beyond the borders of the resort. Actually, by the end of the week, we found the frog noise somewhat comforting, or were too tired to care.

An appropriate plague in Jamaica
would certainly call for deafening tree frogs.

104

Starfish

For three months, Luke had been bartering toys with Ellie by promising to find her a starfish when they got to Jamaica. When we saw a red starfish on the bottom of the ocean, we asked the resort's employee about getting a starfish shell for Ellie.

"No problem," the employee assured us. Later in the cabin we were greeted with someone calling out, "Hello, Mrs. Stewart, we have found two star fish for you. They are dead, so it is all right to take them, but don't unwrap them here on the beach. You should keep them in water or they will smell."

We didn't know what to do with starfish that would smell. We put them on our balcony and opted to leave them there when we packed our suitcase.

Starfish shells make perfect
memories of ocean treasures.

105

Glass Bottom Boat Ride

We took Luke and Beth on a ride in the glass bottom boat. Luke, confined by the cast on his arm, was so pleased to be able to see the ocean life that others had talked about, particularly the ship wreck in the snorkeling area. He knew he saw a pirate's sword and confided that he couldn't wait to tell his sister about it.

It doesn't get much better than a pirate's sword for a five-year-old with one arm in a cast.

Nothing is more enchanting
than a pirate's tale and a ship wreck.

106

Where's the Bell Boy?

Teresa amused us by recounting the paces she was putting her children through to dissipate some of their energy build-up before boarding a plane. First they had a yelling fest—as loud as they could yell for a specified length of time. Then they took turns running around the outside of their house. Two-year-old Zora was quite put out because she was last and had to put on shoes and clothes to run. Friday night was long, indeed, before they boarded the plane.

The children endured a tour of New York City before getting on the ship. Angel, Justin, and Beth were the first ones on the monstrous Carnival Triumph housing 3200 passengers. Teresa's crew couldn't locate a bell boy, so they pulled all their bags including determined Zora who stuck close to Ellie.

Bill and I arranged an appointment to eat lunch with Beth and Ellie. When Zora learned of the date, she informed her mother that she was big too, so we hosted three diners. Zora sat up straight and tall and told me with a twinkle in her eye, "I eat like an adult."

On a cruise ship, children
learn company manners.

107

Crab Racing for Charity

The evening's entertainment for the children was billed as a crab race. I speculated that it would be on the beach, and we would get to chase crabs or cheer for crabs racing to the water. Alas, it was in the auditorium on the dance floor and involved hermit crabs turned loose to race outside a circle. Children were asked to bet money on the crabs. Luke lamented that he would rather chase crabs than watch them.

Parents were consoled by the fact that in teaching children to gamble, half the money would go to a charity in Jamaica.

The lottery takes many forms
in various countries of the world.

108

Beach Party

All food was rolled out and served from a grill at the beach party, a brouhaha that involved a band, a volleyball court, relays in the sand and a limbo contest. The closing entertainment featured a fire dancer. The dancer picked Justin to put the fire tong in his throat. It was a bit daunting for Justin, but he followed directions and was pleased with his success.

The next day we experienced a dinner in the Japanese restaurant. We sat around the grill while a chef cooked and entertained with riddles. The most fun was watching the children use their chopsticks. Of course they entertained themselves by clicking them, making ears out of them, but when the food was ready, eating became serious business. The game plan called for eating everything with chopsticks. I could not imagine a two-year old manipulating chopsticks. With amazing dexterity, Ellie picked up a piece of lettuce with her chopsticks in one hand, lifted the ribbon of lettuce above her head and dropped it in her mouth.

I watched Justin and Luke click their chopsticks and with eyes dancing, poke a ball of rice into their mouths. Beth joined the riddle game, answering the chef's question, "Why did the chicken cross the road, and how did the lollypop cross the road?"

Beth's swift answer cut the waiter short, "It stuck to the chicken." Thank goodness we were too busy for knock-knock jokes!

What wonderful ways we find
to entertain ourselves with food!

109

Seaweed Chips

We explored Canada's oldest city, Saint John, in New Brunswick, and were eager to try dulse in the grocery store, a potato-chip affair made from seaweed, supposedly having medicinal value. We all tried it. If you like eating salty spinach that has a fishy taste, you would like it.

We went to the Bay of Fundy and stopped to see the Reversing Falls Rapids where the highest tide in the world causes the St. John River to reverse direction and flow upstream. Passengers in yellow raincoats with life-jackets and life boats were dipping around in the turbulent water.

Justin wished he had booked the tour, but alas, it was already filled.

It's hard to accept unfamiliar cultural concepts
as normal until we experience them first hand.

110

Hierarchy of Cousins

After dinner, Beth asked quietly if she and Ellie could have their picture taken together. The photographer was ready, and as they assembled, Zora hurriedly joined the group. The picture caught an opportune moment. There is Zora standing so tall, Ellie with her wonderful snaggle-tooth smile, and Beth with a teenage look that says, "It's fun to be in charge."

Pictures capture fleeting moments of history.

111

Belly Dancing

We made arrangements to meet at Bennigan's Grill and get a report on what happened in Disney World with the Kansas City gang.

Zora enjoyed a hands-on-event in which she dressed as a belly dancer and performed for the crowd who stopped to watch. Ellie joined a cooking crew and served cookies.

Small World was the most popular ride, over and over again. Uncle Don gave the girls rides on his shoulders and reported being amused one morning when he picked up Zora in a long dress to find that she had no underwear on. The purchase of Disney World panties saved the day.

Luke reported spending the money he had saved for vacation on a cache of arms. It was too good to be true!

Vacations sometimes necessitate
unusual last minute purchases.

112

A Confiscation of Arms

We surveyed the lush foliage of tropical Florida and watched for alligators in the ditches that lined the highway to the Space Center. The space museum and a three dimensional movie of the astronauts entertained us with the story of their lives in space. Zora loved the glasses that focused the space shuttle in front of her nose. We by-passed the bus tour of the grounds in our eagerness to get on the ship.

Alas, the cache of arms that showed up in Teresa's luggage was confiscated. She had to report to security and learned that all the toy swords, the long play gun, and the plastic hand pistols were placed in confinement. Luke cried, for he had spent his savings on the armaments that he couldn't believe his mother let him buy. Then he remembered that he had put the coin necklace that Uncle Donnie had bought him in the security basket and had forgotten to get it out, or so he thought. Most of the week we grieved and talked about the items. Then he found the necklace in some luggage and protected the medal by wearing it inside his shirt during all meals so that he would not get food on it.

To make a long story short, when we exited the ship, we were given the Disney weapons back, all taped together. To be safe Don put the weapons in his luggage and promised to mail them to Luke to forego any further trouble with the airlines.

The trials we face are often inconsequential
in the big scheme of life.

113

The Silent Drill

We stashed our things away while the children jumped on the beds and made bridges out of the pillows of the couches. Then we had the perfunctory Coast Guard boat drill on deck near the life guard boats.

While passengers ambled in place, Teresa hid out with exhausted Zora in the bathroom. The ship was searched for delinquent passengers who were rousted out for the drill. Zora and her mother rested silently on a towel in the shower and were never found. Cheers!

We learn to follow our government's rules for safety
—usually.

114

The Chocolate Buffet

All eleven of us were seated at a round table near the back of the ship. Our feast began! We tried all kinds of exotic dishes. I could not believe the children devoured things like escargot, clams, cold soups, and foreign dishes. Justin and Zora seemed to like every presentation of salmon.

Don and Justin took in all midnight buffets. Luke was ecstatic about the chocolate buffet. Beth helped Zora and Ellie dance in style at the end of meals with musical presentations by waiters. Teresa and Angel helped the waiters sing "Hoppy Bufday" in multi-lingual style.

The waiters from all around the world found interesting things to tell the diners.

Creative foods are a way
of introducing people to cultural diversity.

115

The Search for Diversions

The ship glided into the port of Nassau, the Capitol City of the Bahamas, but the children found the ship more exciting than the port on a Sunday when shops were shut down.

Glass elevators from the bottom to the top of the ship were a delightful way to zoom up six stories and see all the sights inside and out.

The ultraviolet Arcade room (pronounced "Arcave" by Zora) attracted children and teenagers. It was dark enough to be a cave and kept the younger set out of the casino. Video games were the main attraction.

Justin entertained himself by eating twenty ice cream cones in one day.

Sometimes the ship is better entertainment
than the destination.

116

A Drizzle Castle

We explored the many attractions of Coki Beach.

Justin and Beth rented snorkel equipment that came with a dog bone to attract fish. Luke used snorkel equipment from the grandparents' stash. Zora learned how to make a drizzle sandcastle under Don's tutelage. Sand was scooped up from the water and dribbled on the massive castle site. Beth and Ellie took time out to have their hair French braided under a tree beside a bucket of conch shells that two little boys had dredged up and sold to the proprietor of the braiding business. The adults watched out for the safety of children splashing in the gentle waves, a quiet and restful grandparents' pastime. The massive drizzle castle was recorded on film and left on the beach to entertain future tourists.

We were forced to learn the value
of contributing to public art.

117

The Mustache Dinner

We took a water taxi to Philipsburg, St. Maarten to swim on another beach and were impressed with the new island. Zora came back to the ship after two hours of swimming to eat and take a nap, which of course, she didn't need.

Our family entered the ship's scavenger hunt and traipsed around the ship looking for clues, assured that with eleven family members we would have no trouble winning the sack of goodies. Other family groups participated and, unfortunately, none of our names were drawn.

We got out our own stash of toys—punching balls, pick-up sticks, rockets, mustaches, and books. Mustaches became the proper attire for dinner.

Imaginative play calls for creative action.

118

Smile if You Love Me

We met in Miami to board our ship for the Caribbean. We had the boarding routine down pat. All participated in the lifeboat drill. At a round table, all eleven of us played games while we waited for food. We tried making someone smile by saying, "I don't have time to talk to you, but smile if you love me honey." Zora snidely retorted, "I'll smile, but I don't love you, honey."

We entertain ourselves throughout life
by playing with words.

119

The Hypnotic Performance

Our first port of call was Half Moon Cay, a private island for Carnival Cruises. We found the island landscaped with water slides and tethered animals in the water for the children to climb on. A band played on the beach for limbo competition; swimmers hunted for shells and fed bananas to translucent fish. We were able to locate one another with our yellow hats, courtesy of Pa.

During the evening's show, Teresa's children learned about hypnotism. A hypnotist demonstrated his art by choosing members from the audience to hypnotize. Teresa was among those chosen, and proved to be an amusing and entertaining actress.

Don gave Justin juggling lessons. We then endured his juggling balls over our beds and our heads—more exciting than the entertainer of the evening.

Family fun goes off in many
directions on a cruise.

120

Zip-lining in Skagway

While Don was honing his canoeing skills at a glacier in Alaska, Angel rounded up a zip-line crew of the four older children to hike up a mountain and attempt the daring feat of zipping through the trees on a cable, gaining a first-hand view of Alaska from the tree tops. It was Skagway's attempt to entertain the tourists in a village only four blocks wide and twenty-three blocks long, just a foothold in a gigantic wilderness. Only Ellie was too light to sail across the wide expanse and had to have a boost midway, quite pleased with the attention. The rest of the zip-liners negotiated the feat with style and reported on the escapade at supper, feeling courageous and smug. They managed to make it through the main course before vacating the dining room for a bed. The climb up the mountain took care of all their extra steam.

Zora had waited patiently for "an adventure with Angel." When they returned from zip-lining, she gallivanted off with Angel and Beth to pan for gem stones, and at supper triumphantly reported of having found a cache.

We expanded our understanding of our earth
by exploring its unfamiliar wildernesses.

121

Zora's Song

We were interrupted in our choice of entertainment activities on the ship, when Luke appeared and invited the parental units to the children's show. We rushed off to hear Zora sing "Tomorrow" a cappella from *Annie*. We watched Ellie, in teacher style, explain a trick our waiter had used as entertainment at our dining table. Some children played the piano, some did gymnastics, and one little boy bounced a ball all over the stage.

We learned all kinds of data about whales—that whales are playful; that a whale's milk is the texture of tooth paste; that singing is done by the males; and that each species of whale sings its own song. We were pleased to learn that whales seek out human company, especially when someone imitates their song. Interesting!

If Zora were a whale would she
sing a song we would understand?

122

Just Remembering

Justin

"When I was born I had awful colic, and Neanie would put me on the dryer, which jiggled and hummed and kept my tummy warm, so I didn't have to cry. Walking up and down the stairs helped, because I knew someone was doing something for me."

"My Dad had a hard time sleeping in the room with my bassinet, 'cause the noises I made kept him awake, so I got to go to the basement and make all the sighs and sounds I wanted."

"I have cleaned my closet, and I know everyone will want to see ALL the pieces of my pirate ship. I found every one of them."

"My art work needs to be hung up where people can appreciate it—every piece of it."

"Being a piñata in the school program was wonderful fun 'cause I got to throw candy at the kids."

"All we can have for Fourth of July at Pa and Neanie's house are smoke bombs and cackling chickens, because all the policemen are guarding the town of Columbia from explosions."

"I hid my chewed bubble gun under my car seat, so now I have gum to chew anytime I want. I just remember not to chew the gum under the seats at the movies."

"Plastic worms are more fun in a bathtub than real ones, 'cause we don't have to be afraid of them."

"I am so hungry after school. I can eat a whole cheeseburger and a milk shake on the way home."

"There's one way to get away from Baby Beth playing with my toys. I get in the playpen. She can play on the floor."

"You can see me ride a bike at Pa's house because Pa pushed me until I learned."

"My eyes stay open when I swim with goggles, and I can see what's on the bottom of the ocean."

"I get to sleep with Dad when Mama is on call at the hospital, even if it isn't thundering."

"If you come to school, you can see me get across the new parallel bars without falling off."

"Bring a big sack when you come to the downtown parade because you will need it to pick up all the candy."

"I brought a 'note' home for you, Mama. I made it all by myself in music class."

"Soccer games are wonderful. I get to run and run and run and sometime kick."

"I waded by myself in a big ditch on the farm and found a big stick and lots of gooey mud."

"At the Fair we went through cow barns, horse barns, rabbit barns, chicken barns and goat barns and ate Pa's caramel corn."

"It takes a whole bottle of Windex for me to clean the bathroom, if my nanny is not watching."

"I love being a reporter on a cruise ship—what's on the menu, where the ice cream machine is and who is reading and who is taking a nap."

Elizabeth

"On the soccer team I stay away from kids who are trying to kick the ball so I won't get kicked. It's more fun to swing on the goal post, anyhow, but I'm not supposed to do that when the game is going on."

"Neanie has a dish-towel rack in her kitchen, and I pull off all the towels and put them in the floor. Now she sews buttons on all her towels. It's no fun anymore."

"I eat yogurt with a spoon, but I use my hand to put the yogurt in the spoon so I can get most of it in my mouth."

"The sand-box Pa built is wonderful. I dig holes and fill them up with water and sometimes put my feet in the holes."

"When I heard about the war, I packed my suitcase so I could be ready if they called Mama to serve as a doctor. Mama stopped me when I started to pack for Justin even though he wouldn't pack for himself."

"I can't help it, but my thumb makes me feel better when I get sleepy."

"Mama's computer ran off invitations for my pony-riding birth-day party. Mama said she would mail them, but I found them in her desk, and I thought I should take them to school because they might get lost in the mail. I got stopped. No one listens to me."

"I love to play with ice, but my hands get so cold they hurt. Justin told me to shake them. I have to shake my whole body to get the job done."

"Walking in a walker with new shoes is such fun. I go so fast."

"Everybody was surprised when I swam across the lake with Mama. She let me rest along the way, but I made it."

"I can turn somersaults on my water trampoline, and most of the time I stay on it."

"We went on a field trip with Justin to a 'Lolly-pop and Peanut-butter Concert.' I didn't think I would like it, but I did. I learned how to clap."

Luke

"I had to be fished out of my mother in the operating room, and I protested every minute. But I came out looking pretty good, so they say, all because my nose and chin were sticking out the wrong way. I wasn't mashed up because of something called labor."

"I spent the first night at home being rocked all night in a big stuffy chair. When my sock cap slid off, I fretted 'till Neanie put it back on my head to keep me warm. I didn't have much hair. She's learning how to rock me to get rid of the hiccoughs and poked a pacifier at me when I cry. An upright position is more comfortable for my full tummy. I sighed so she would know I was around to be loved."

"Playing money with a jar of pennies and a scoop truck is so much fun, but I don't put the monies in my ears or mouth."

"My foot feels like it's fizzing inside my skin. Mama says it is sleeping."

"On our cruise we fed bananas to fish you could see through."

"Well, I slept in Uncle Don's closet 'cause I had trouble sleeping in a strange room. Now I have come out of the closet."

"Getting ready for school is such a pain. I have an acorn for 'A' in my back-pack, but I can't find my shoes. 'Oh, Luke, they are on your feet,' my mama told me."

"My big-boy bed bounces and jiggles and has fire-engine sheets, but sometimes I forget I can get out of my bed all by myself."

"You can play bear with me, and we can roll on the carpet and tumble and growl. It's really fun."

I have my hand raised up so I can talk. I need the door. Mama said, 'No, Luke, you mean the floor.'"

"Well, I want to read this book, and I can't do it with my eyes shut. I don't want to go to sleep. It's a problem."

"Beth calls me 'Woot.' My name is Luke, but I'll call her Beth anyway."

Eleanor is having a confrontation with her new shoes. Guess I'll have to help her."

143

Eleanor

"After I put lotion on my legs, arms and face, I nice and soft."

"I can blow out my candles fast 'cause I'm not so old."

"I like climbing trees hanging upside down. It makes me feel like a monkey."

"On a cruise ship I fly up the stairs and beat the elevator."

"My toasted cheese sandwich was crusty on the outside and warm and gooey inside. I pulled it apart and put it on my head and told Mom it was a hat. She didn't think it was funny."

"Diddle Cat likes to sleep with me. He feels so soft."

"I prowl for cookies that Mama hides, but I can find them."

"Having my hair French braided on our cruise made my hair hurt."

"I am good at feeding myself spaghetti. I don't need any of Neanie's help. She has trouble letting me do it by myself."

"I learned to feed myself with chopsticks when I was two. Sometimes I missed."

"I got an American Girl doll that looked just like me, even dressed like me."

"In Grade School I got to sing in 'Beauty and the Beast' and be a spoon. It was fun."

"Was I ever excited when Mama got me a little baby sister. She couldn't even sit up and slept most of the time. Everybody came to see her and Mama even let me hold her, but she mainly just lopped. She got so she could smile at me when I entertained."

"I play violin in the orchestra of my school. My teacher had me sit in the first chair seat. I was so surprised and happy."

"I was selected to play in the Youth Symphony of Kansas City and wore a long black skirt. I looked so grown-up."

Zora

"Mama says Luke and Ellie want to be Venus Fly Traps for Halloween, and I can be a fly."

"I'm only seven months old, but I can pinch Neanie's nose, and she will wake up. Then we'll get up."

"Turning on the water hose in the sand-box is more fun than shoveling sand."

"When the kids laugh, I laugh big and loud even if I don't know what they laugh about."

"It is nice to sleep with someone and find them with my feet.

"Pa and I are really good at working puzzle books."

"I play 'I Spy Stories' on Neanie and Pa's old computer. I am good at finding things."

"A jelly fish bit me on a cruise, but I didn't cry much."

"I danced on the window sill of the cruise ship and in the isles with the waiters. They like me".

"When I was born I had black hair that covered my head and even the rims of my ears, so Mama said."

"Everybody wants to feed me, but I'd rather feed myself, even if I make a mess."

"I like hats. Sometimes people make me hats. Sometimes I make hats, and sometimes I wear other peoples' hats that make me look snazzy. Neanie made me a lion's hat and a dress with a tail."

"I learned how to clap my hands when Luke and Ellie entertained me. They liked my clapping."

"We go to Columbia and watch parades. Sometimes they throw out candy for us. I like that. Sometimes they ride funny little cars and big bicycles."

"I'm pretty good at blowing out candles on birthdays, 'cause my mama and I have the same birthday. We blow out candles together, but we don't have to share our presents."

"Uncle Don helped me make a sand castle on the beach It

was almost as tall as I was. We left it for everyone to see."

"I have always liked to entertain people, making funny faces, silly hands, and crazy poses."

"I got to be a Munchkin in 'The Wizard of Oz.' We practiced for two weeks but I didn't get tired. It lasted two hours. I wore a hat and danced and sang and talked. I am ready to carry on with drama."

"In the Highland's Variety Show I dressed up like a duck and played the piano. No one knew it was me unless they read the program. People give performers flowers. What fun!"

May we become wiser for having experienced our children's observations.

The ☆Old
Yellow Couch

123

The Old Yellow Couch

As adults we take in the wonderment of life and learn from its mysteries. I should like to share a mystery that I wrote down in 1997 after it happened to me. I could not talk about it at the time. I share what I learned from this experience as I have learned through my grandchildren's search for knowledge.

It was early in the morning. My sister Ruth and her husband David were staying with us while he sought medical help at Boone Hospital in Columbia, Missouri for esophageal cancer. Ruth left early for the hospital. My husband Bill was still asleep. I sat alone on the old yellow couch in the family room and started my morning devotions with a heavy heart. So much troubled me. My brother-in-law, David Richardson, was courageously taking medication for a tumor in his esophagus, waiting to see whether the tests would show if he were a good candidate for a surgery that would pull his stomach up and by-pass the tumor. Would he have an opportunity for the operation that would buy him time?

By a dim light I started reading, praying, and crying. I heard a voice speak words in an unknown tongue. The words came from beside me on the other end of the couch. I turned to look, but no one was there. An audible voice had spoken distinctly in a foreign language, yet immediately I understood the words. They were real.

"I will be with you." There was never any doubt who spoke the words, never any doubt what they meant. Jesus had spoken. Would anyone believe me?

The mystery of Jesus goes beyond the grave. He crosses the barrier of life back and forth, revealing God. When I read of Pentecost, I read of the babble of tongues, but every one hears in his own language. How can that be? I don't understand. I just know that Jesus said, "I will be with you."

When I read the biblical account of the Walk to Emmaus, I read of Jesus explaining his life and death to two men walking on the Emmaus road. His presence was real, but after conversation and breaking bread, He vanished.

When I read of Paul's conversion experience, I read about a man who did not know Jesus personally but responded to His voice and a bright light. The experience was so powerful that Paul's whole life was redirected.

I reflect that an old yellow couch is an unlikely place for Jesus to speak to me. I was startled. I understand why the Bible describes the terror of the disciples about things they did not understand. I remember that after healing a leper, Jesus said, "Tell no man, but show yourself to the priest for a testimony." I could not talk about my experience that morning. Sometime later, I told my husband Bill about the mysterious event.

Shortly after David's death, I was diagnosed with mono-clonal-gammopathy and underwent six months of plasma-pheresis and chemotherapy. I lived with Jesus' words, "I will be with you." I was not afraid.

The mystery of creation, of birth, of death, and of the intricacies of our bodies with a soul is something we don't understand. I sat in a hospital room while the doctor explained a delicate procedure to Bill about taking out his parathyroid gland, showing it on a computer screen and describing how it worked in an interconnected way within our bodies. I felt strangely moved by how miraculously our bodies are put together by a God whose love envelopes us and walks with us into eternity. I felt moved by the doctor who explained the process with such quiet awe.

We treasure each moment we have to live with God and His children. Others have heard God's voice through the ages. We are moved by their witness.

One night I awoke hearing the words to a song confirming

what I had experienced. I got up in the night, went to the piano bench, and found the hymn that affirmed my experience as I was affirmed by my grandchildren's experiences.

"I serve a Risen Savior; He's in the world today.
I know that he is living, whatever foes may say.
I see his hand of mercy; I hear his voice of cheer,
And just the time I need him, he's always near.
He lives. He lives. Christ Jesus lives today!
He walks with me and talks with me along life's narrow way.
He lives. He lives, salvation to impart.
You ask me how I know he lives. He lives within my heart."
— Alfred Ackley, 1933

God has created our world to function on love. May we and our children reach out to understand the nature of giving and receiving His love.

CPSIA information can be obtained at www.ICGtesting.com
Printed in the USA
LVOW051603210413

330130LV00002B/18/P